Losing Butch

A Novelette Based on a Real Life

John P. Choisser

The names of the characters have all been changed.

ISBN 978-1534836303

www.johnchoisser.com

Published by Readerplace, Inc.

San Diego, California, U.S.A.

www.readerplace.com

To hear the song of the Mourning Dove, go to
https://www.allaboutbirds.org/guide/Mourning_Dove/sounds.

Contents

Dedication

To Jessica

Prologue

The three of us sat around the small round table in Jessica's kitchen, with the pendant light illuminating the box of papers and photos. As the afternoon gradually became evening, the rest of the house receded into darkness around us. Our hands, faces, and voices seemed isolated from the rest of the world.

Family photos, typical and yet very personal, were taken from the box, and handed between us as Jesse told story after story regarding the way it had been. What a good big sister Deena had been. How bright both kids were, and what great friends they had. High school proms and graduations. Church choirs and service clubs. Scholarships for both Deena and Butch at the university three years apart.

"They were such good kids," whispered Jessica, "Everything was just perfect."

Though related, we had all grown up in different cities, and saw each other rarely. Some of the stories I had heard from my father, and some things I knew first hand. But there was much I didn't know, and some things I would never know or fully understand.

"John," Jessica said quietly, "you're the best writer in the family. After we're all gone, I hope you will tell this story in the hopes it will help somebody somewhere."

There are a lot of gaps I had fill in, but here, to the best of my recollection, is Butch's story.

Chapter 1. Early Days

The Mourning Dove had been a part of Butch's life as long as he could remember. Its soft song would send him to sleep at night and wake him in the mornings: Coo-ah, coo, coo, coo. Coo-ah, coo, coo, coo.

This morning was Christmas morning during his junior year of high school. It was the morning he got his briefcase. It became his tangible companion that accompanied his dream of becoming an attorney.

His grades were very good, and everyone in the family expected him to earn an academic scholarship to the University of Arizona, where his uncle Roger had graduated from law school many years before.

Butch's vision went beyond there. Since his boyhood days, he had enjoyed visiting his uncles Roger and Joseph in their law offices in downtown Phoenix. The office was located front and center on the second floor of the Luhrs Tower, one of the only tall buildings downtown back then, and just a few blocks from the courthouse. Butch often visualized watching a sign artist painting his name on the frosted glass door beside those of his uncles. Beautiful gold letters with a thin black outline. Elegant.

When he took the tan leather briefcase out of its wrapping, he immediately noticed his initials embossed in gold right above the handle. "I'll keep this forever," he thought to himself, "through my whole legal career."

After photos and a noisy and happy family Christmas breakfast, the four of them, Jim, Jessica, Deena and Butch, went to church as usual. Butch and Deena were both in the choir, and enjoyed singing their favorite seasonal hymns.

Butch proudly told his friend Mark about his briefcase, and Mark was duly impressed.

"Real leather?" Mark asked.

"Yes, and with my initials right above the handles," was Butch's reply.

"In gold?" Mark's eyes widened.

"Yes, real gold," Butch said. "Come over this afternoon to see it."

So later in the day, with the living room cleaned up after the gift-opening mess, Mark stopped by to examine Butch's new treasure.

They explored the compartments, and put paper and pencils in places that were designed for them. The pleasant smell of the leather and the smooth luxurious feel spurred visions of the future whirling through Butch's head. He saw himself walking from the office to the elevator with the briefcase. Down the elevator with a beautiful assistant at his side, and across the street, and further down the block to the courthouse, with the important papers stowed safely in his impressive briefcase. Into the courtroom, laying the briefcase on the table, and beginning by addressing the court in a confidant voice. All that could be just a few years away!

Butch (actually Jim, Jr.) continued to excel in the classroom and on the field. He enjoyed sports, but valued his studies more. By the time he was a senior he had a steady girlfriend, who was a year behind him in school. Butch and Amy were together a lot. They went to movies, inexpensive dates, the local drive in, church, youth council, and choir.

When graduation day came and went, Butch, like all his friends, started his summer job to accumulate some money to help with college. He had long worked part time at the local grocery store, stocking shelves, sweeping floors, and bagging groceries. Now full-time for the summer, he worked his way up to the produce department, where he unpacked and prepared produce for the store displays. His father Jim had been a farmer, and Butch always thought he had some farm genes. He enjoyed the look, smell, and feel of the fruits and vegetables, and kept them fresh in the cold counters by spraying water on them every hour.

Work, Amy, family, church, and swimming at the municipal pool filled the days of summer, which practically flew by.

Many years ago Jim had sold his farm, and moved to the city when the kids were small. He took a job at a large local tire dealership, and worked his way up to be the general manager. Now their home was in a nice upper-middle class neighborhood where all the neighbors knew each other.

The local kids had all grown up playing together, outside in the winter, and inside during the summer heat. Girl games, boy games, nobody seemed to care. Butch was good at Jacks and Pick-Up Sticks and the girls were equally good at cowboys and war games. The Saturday movie was the treat for the week, and for the following week everyone wanted to be like the hero the preceding Saturday, whether it was a carrier pilot, a cowboy, or a famous detective.

Amy was only a year younger than Butch, and it wasn't until their teen years that a little romance sparked. Until then they had been more like siblings, with Butch, Amy, Deena, and the other neighborhood kids all together most of the time.

Butch took the boyfriend-girlfriend relationship a little more seriously than Amy did. Amy knew she wasn't nearly the intellectual equal of Butch and Deena, and probably would get married and start a family soon after high school. Butch, of course, had his mind set on college and law school, and vaguely hoped that Amy would still be around if and when the time came sometime in the distant future. He also realized that she was average in the scholastic area, but, well, she was as cute as they came, a cheerleader, and had a very appealing outgoing personality.

When the time came for Butch to go to college, they agreed that each could date others. Nevertheless, Butch held on to the hope that Amy could be his someday.

The day came for packing up to leave for Tucson, and Butch had his suitcase open on the living room floor while everyone, it seemed, participated in what he would take and what he would leave. The University of Arizona in Tucson was a good choice for Butch. It was far enough away from home so that he was "leaving home" after high school, but at 120 miles or so, was close enough that he could easily come home on holidays and for summer work.

Deena was already in Tucson, starting her third year, so it was only Jim, Jessica, and Butch that piled in the family car for the trip south. Butch had carefully packed his admission papers and other important documents and supplies in his precious briefcase, and placed it on the seat next to him, underneath a duffle bag of clothes and other stuff. Amy tearfully waved goodbye as the car pulled away from the curb, made a U-turn, and headed for the highway.

Chapter 2. Tucson

Jake put his dusty boots up against the porch railing and pushed his chair back against the wall. He gently stirred the bourbon and water with his forefinger, enjoying the tinkle of the ice in the glass.

The sun was getting low on the horizon, and the desert was beginning to glow from a typical spectacular Arizona sunset. His weather-beaten handsome face had seen many of these, but every one of them was different.

He wondered how many more years he could ride his fences. The repairs were constant now, as the illegal foot traffic from the border came north through his ranch constantly. He smiled as he thought to himself that maybe he should put in a gate. One with a sign that asked people to "Please close the gate behind you." In Spanish.

Maybe it's time to buy an ATV and retire my horse, he thought.

He was enjoying watching the sunset from his porch, while the bourbon warmed his body and eased the aches from a day in the saddle. Pleasant smells came through the screen door from the kitchen as Irma cooked dinner.

He squinted into the sunset as he noticed the headlights in the distance. The lights caught his eye as they seemed to wink on and off as the car drove in and out of the dips in the dirt road, the lights growing brighter as they got closer.

Kind of fast, Jake thought, for a corduroy dirt road, where the traction was poor even in the driest weather. The tires tend to skip along the tops of the ridges at higher speeds, making the car wander and slide.

Desert Corduroy Road

Must not be a local driver. Probably some college kids coming back from a party in the desert, no doubt underage and half (or more) drunk.

Then the sound came, and he knew it was bad, real bad. The sound of the crash wasn't that of a car leaving the road and plowing into the sand or a bunch of prickly pears. No, the sound was of steel hitting rock, and the rock always won.

Jake opened the screen door, grabbed the pickup keys off the nail, and shouted to Irma in the kitchen to call Dave to get help. The wreck would be just south of their ranch road, and would be easy to find. Irma was already talking to the sheriff's office as Jake turned his truck down the road on its way to the scene.

As Jake expected, the wreck was pretty bad. The station wagon was upright, resting on its wheels, but the top was crushed in as if by a giant fist. Inside was a yelling, screaming mass of arms and legs, some moving, some still. Jake couldn't even tell how many kids were in there. But he could smell the beer. And one young man in the back had his head sandwiched between the beer keg and the caved-in roof of the car. He wasn't moving. "Oh, man," Jake thought to himself, "This kid's a goner."

Jim drove as fast as he dared, covering the distance between Phoenix and Tucson in a little over an hour and a half, reversing the trip that they had made only two days before. The police hadn't been very specific, only telling them that Butch was critically injured and was in the ER at Tucson General Hospital. Jim and Jessica hardly talked, both having trouble believing that only a few days before they had driven this road in the other direction, after dropping off Butch and his stuff at the dormitory.

What a contrast. On the way home, just day before yesterday, they both felt very assured and proud. Both of their children were successes. Deena was beginning her last year, an honor student, and was accepted at the University of California Davis to get her veterinary degree. She had gotten the most possible out of her undergraduate college career, being elected a member of the Spurs honorary her second year on campus. Being an officer in her sorority plus her other activities didn't keep her from getting grades good enough to keep her annual scholarship that paid her tuition. And now she was engaged, planning to get married before moving to California.

And Butch. Also graduated from high school with honors, and also had an academic scholarship to help with tuition. He was just starting his college career that was intended to end with him becoming a law partner with his uncles. He had taken his precious briefcase he had received for graduation with him to the university as a reminder of the goals he had set for himself.

And now they weren't sure he would live through the night.

Chapter 3. In the ER

When they arrived, Deena was already sitting by Butch's bedside, holding one of his hands. Nearly his whole head was wrapped in bandages, except for one closed eye, and his nose and mouth were sprouting hoses and tubes.

He was motionless, but the monitors and scopes showed lots of activity, at least for now. Discussions with the doctors and nurses were discouraging, however, because they suspected very serious brain trauma. Scans were scheduled, and surgery was on alert to remove some skull as soon as the surgeon arrived to relieve the brain swelling.

One of the sheriff's deputies was standing by, to give the family a report on the accident. Although the investigation was not nearly complete, how Butch was injured was clear.

He had been riding in the back of the station wagon with the nearly empty beer keg, since all the seats were filled with other students. His 6 foot 3 inch body was curled up just to fit in the back. When the car left the road and overturned, Butch's head was caught between the keg and the car's roof when the boulder smashed it in. Smashed in another inch and they would all be meeting in a different facility.

Although there were others injured, none of them was nearly as serious as Butch. The driver had obviously been drinking, as were all the others. Sure enough, the driver was from out of state, and not used to driving on the dry corduroy roads of the desert. He didn't know they could feel as slick as ice at high speeds, and that, combined with the loss of traction coming out of one of the frequent dips in the road, loss of control was easy.

After what seemed like an eternity, the surgeon arrived and Butch was taken for scans and surgery. Jim, Jessica and Deena sat in the waiting room half paralyzed with fear and grief. They prayed together, both silently and aloud.

Soon Jim's brothers Roger and Joseph arrived from Phoenix, along with Amy, to join the family as they waited for the doctors and Butch to emerge from surgery. The doctors hadn't given the family much hope, given the seriousness of the injury.

After what seemed like an eternity, a doctor emerged through the swinging doors with a stern look on his face. The family held their breaths as the doctor said, "I think he's going to make it." After a collective sigh of relief, he went on, "He is hurt very badly. I don't know how much mental capacity he is going to recover."

The fear and dread swept over them like a wave. Mental capacity? What is he saying?

"Let's all sit down," the doctor said to the family. "He's not paralyzed, and I'm not too worried about that. But frankly, I'm not sure how badly some other functions might be affected."

"Like what?" asked Jim.

"Speech, coordination, reasoning, emotions. I think his vision is going to be OK, and so is his hearing. We'll learn a lot in the next few days," the doctor replied. "But I think you should be prepared for a long and difficult rehabilitation, which might not achieve much."

Chapter 4. Beginning a New Life

So began a long, difficult journey. Butch had control of his movements, and could feed himself within a few days. But his speech was very juvenile, as were his emotions. He seemed to be mentally transported back in time to his early years.

Much of his previous extensive vocabulary was gone, and he initially had trouble even recognizing family members. Even when recognized, he seemed to need to re-learn their names. But he made progress.

Could he ever return to his former self? That was far from clear. He had been able to return to Phoenix within a fairly short time, and control of his care was transferred to St. Joseph's Hospital there. He spent hours and hours in rehab, where he and other patients worked on their individual recovery programs.

When Butch was able to live again at home, Jim began the routine of taking Fridays off from his management job at the tire dealership to spend time with Butch. Butch treasured these days, looking forward to them all week, crossing each day off his calendar.

However Butch became very depressed as he began to recognize the apparently permanent change that had happened in his life. The psychiatrist prescribed anti-depressant drugs to help him cope with the growing realization that he might never be an attorney after all.

An important part of Butch's therapy were activities that exercised his brain – things like keeping lists, counting things, and, above all, collecting and organizing things. It didn't seem to matter what, but Jim and Butch soon got involved in coin collecting, an activity that they could do together. Many Fridays were spend exploring shops, examining coins, and checking their lists to see what additions they needed to add to the collection.

Jim and Jessica developed a long term strategy that they followed to bring Butch back as nearly as possible to his prior abilities. The plan consisted of gradually increasing the difficulty or complexity of activities. Building Butch's self-reliance and independence was also important, in the hopes that he could someday enjoy an independent life away from home.

The hospital continued to engage Butch in its rehab program. Though mentally injured, he had maintained his stature and physical size, and became a leader in the rehab groups. Mental exercises, counting, sorting, reading, and writing all were part of the program. Managing collections of things was a good way to engage patients in several of these exercises at once.

One day, Butch discovered a great collection project, which he excitedly shared with the others in his rehab class. Campbell's Soup was giving things to schools in return for labels off of their soup cans. His group adopted the plan, and Butch began his own collection at home.

He quickly discovered that labels from home would never amount to much. But the trash bins of the old folks' home a few blocks away became a virtual gold mine.

It seemed a good idea at the time.

Even though Butch was making slow progress in his rehab program, other aspects of his life didn't go as well.

Chapter 5. Losing Amy

Amy couldn't stop the tears. She sat in the living room with Jim and Jessica, and struggled to come up with the words. But Jim and Jessica knew what was wrong, and they found ways to help. They knew it was more than her sadness for Butch's injury.

Amy came over at a time she knew Butch was out gathering empty soup cans.

"I'm so sorry for Butch, and I love him so much," she blubbered. "But all these months – I just don't see – I mean – he *is* making a *little* progress."

"Honey," Jessica said, "you are like a part of the family. We know and love you, too. But that doesn't mean that you and Butch need to be a couple."

"No, I mean, I had hoped for a normal family. I'm sorry, I don't mean "normal", well, I can't…"

Jim interrupted. "Amy, we feel like parents to you. We know what you mean. Butch might never lead a normal life, and you don't need to become a caregiver, especially at your age. It's OK."

"I've been dating Bruce," Amy confessed. "He wants to get serious. I don't know if that makes it better or worse."

"Of course we know Bruce, and he is a wonderful young man," Jessica said, "And he's already moving up the management chain at his dad's business. If you and he can make a happy home, go for it."

"No, I mean, well, OK, I guess." Amy couldn't bring herself to make the decision, but she knew she had to.

The three of them hugged, and Amy left, still wiping her eyes.

A few minutes later, Butch walked in and asked, "Was that Amy's car that just left?"

Jim and Jessica glanced at each other. "Yes," Jim said, "she was only here for a few minutes."

"Why didn't she wait for me?" Butch asked. "She knows my schedule."

"Honey, come here," said Jessica, patting the sofa next to her. "Amy is very upset and we have to help her. Understand her. Can we talk about this?"

"I know," Butch said, his face clouding over. "She doesn't love me anymore." His lower lip started to quiver.

"Oh Butch, honey," Jessica said, "Put your head in my lap and we'll talk."

Butch did as she asked, and Jessica began to speak.

"You and Amy had a lot of dreams, didn't you?"

"Yes," Butch responded, "and we still do."

"Now your dreams have changed, haven't they?
And have her dreams changed, too?" Jessica asked.

"I still dream of becoming a lawyer," Butch said.
"in the office with Uncle Roger and Uncle Joseph.
With my briefcase. On the second floor of the Luhrs
Tower. Right down the street from the courthouse."

"Son," Jim said, "you realize that you have a lot of
recovery to do first, don't you? And that it's already
been a long time and it will take still longer?"

"Sure, Dad," Butch said, "But I'm managing my
collections really well, I've already got 854 soup
cans, and maybe someday I can drive again."

"Honey, let's think of Amy for a minute, OK?"
suggested Jessica.

"I think about her all the time already," Butch
responded.

"Amy needs to have her own family, with a nice
house and children, and someday grandchildren,"
Jessica said. "We love her so much; don't we want
her to be happy? Shouldn't we do whatever we can
to make her dreams come true, also?"

"Sure," Butch said, "let's make her happy."

"OK, then," Jim said, "you two already agreed to date other people, right?"

"That was while I was in college," Butch said, "I'm not now, I'm home again."

"But there are things she needs that you and we can't provide for her now," Jessica explained. "It might be a long time before you can work to support her. Don't you want to work and earn money so you can buy her nice things?"

"I can't," replied Butch.

"I know," Jessica said, "So we have to let her go to find a new life. OK?"

"OK, but when I'm well again, I'll marry her," Butch announced.

"Honey, by then she might already be married," Jessica said.

"Maybe there is someone else meant for you, Son," Jim added.

"No, it's her," Butch insisted. "I have to go now."

With that he stood up, and went purposefully to his room, shut the door, picked up Amy's picture off of his dresser, threw it in the wastebasket, lay down on his bed, and cried.

And the Mourning Dove sang as if trying to console him with its soft, sad song: Coo-ah, coo, coo, coo.

Chapter 6. The Yellow Mustang

One of the skills that Butch worked hard to regain was the ability to drive a car. The mental quickness and physical dexterity were initially hard to come by, but with many hours spent in empty parking lots with his dad, Butch began to handle the family Ford sedan pretty well. Jim and Butch looked forward to the time Butch could get his license; an important step toward independence.

Finally the day came when it was time for Butch to go to the state office to apply for his license. The idea was for him to just quietly renew his old license so the written and driving tests could be avoided. It wasn't clear that he would actually be able to pass either one of those.

It worked, and although the old license had expired, Butch looked enough like himself in the old license to get the renewal. The golf ball size dent in his right temple wasn't that noticeable.

Right away Jim took Butch shopping for an affordable used car, and found the perfect one: a classic yellow Ford Mustang. It needed some fixing up, but that would be another thing that they could do together.

Jim sat in the passenger seat as Butch became acquainted with the location of the controls, and adjusted the seat and mirrors. Jim thought it was best if Butch drove the car around the lot a few times before venturing out onto the road, and after a few hesitant mistakes, controlled the car well enough so Jim decided that Butch could drive the car home.

Jessica was at the kitchen sink looking out the front window, and saw Jim pull into the driveway, followed by Butch in the Mustang. She ran out to greet them, and as Jim stopped his car in the driveway, Butch, waving and smiling at his mother, ran into the back of Jim's stopped car.

"Well," Jim thought to himself, "we'll have to work on Butch getting distracted while driving. He's getting a little better little by little," he told himself.

Butch named his car Elmer.

Chapter 7. Short Careers

Jim and Jessica agreed with one of Butch's therapists that Butch's struggle toward normalcy would be helped if he had a job. It seemed like a good idea, and Butch thought it might be fun.

So Jim called his friends and contacts for ideas, and between them they hatched a plan. Start simple, and see if he could gradually advance in capability toward more meaningful jobs.

Jim had already had discussions with brothers Roger and Joseph, and none of them could think of a way Butch could be of any help in the law offices. His struggles to re-learn the alphabet made filing chores impossible, and difficulty in writing ruled out telephone answering and appointment booking.

One of their other friends owned a restaurant, and he thought that maybe Butch could start out as a bus boy, and perhaps work his way up to more responsible jobs. The restaurant was only a mile away from home, and was an easy trip for Butch and Elmer, his Mustang.

Everybody loved Butch, as you might expect of a friendly, outgoing man-child. Simple and polite, courteous and always smiling, he appeared to have real promise as a customer-pleasing worker. However, his lack of physical coordination and wandering attention caused problems from the beginning.

One of the first accidents happened on the first day. Butch, with an armload of dirty dishes, was distracted by a pretty girl in shorts sitting at the counter. He then ran smack into the back of a waiter, who then dropped his cargo over the table and its guests.

The owner began to worry that Butch's mishaps might get to be more expensive than broken dishes. He began to be concerned about liability problems; customer and employee safety are an important consideration in the food service business, and carelessness can be very harmful and expensive.

After a few weeks, it became pretty clear that Butch could not continue at the restaurant, and so Jim had to break the news to Butch that he wasn't going to be working there any more.

So Butch went back to his full-time collecting job, filling Elmer's trunk each day with his special version of trash, which he sorted and stored in the driveway at home.

Chapter 8. The Driveway

The family now consisted just of Jessica, Jim, and Butch, since Deena had married after college and moved to California. She was happy and busy working on her veterinary degree at UC Davis, and looking forward to a career that would allow her useful self-employment while planning on raising a family in the future.

Jessica, Jim, and Butch lived in a nice middle-class area of Phoenix with typical ranch-style homes. The homes had generous sized lots, and because of the benign weather, had carports instead of garages.

Ranch Style Home with Carport

The carport was a great place for Butch to store his collection of things. One section was for newspapers, another for small boxes containing treasures like colorful pieces of broken glass and pottery, and another for his growing collection of magazines, which he would go through hour by hour sitting in a lawn chair sandwiched in between his stuff and the front of the family car.

The Mustang had been relegated to parking on the street in front of the house, since, as usually is the case, the wrong car was always in front when they were both in the driveway. An additional problem was that as Butch's collection of stuff grew, the family car no longer could pull all the way into the carport, and was gradually being edged out toward the street as the weeks and months went by.

Butch's organizing the soup can movement had been a great success. All the patients in the class were now collecting soup can labels and bringing them to the meetings, where they got sorted and counted.

So the project grew, and every week Butch would bring home a stack of labels the others had collected that he would count, sort and file in shoe boxes in the driveway.

He enlisted the help of Elmer, going exploring for likely places to find empty cans. After an afternoon of collecting, he would empty the cans out of his trunk into the driveway. Before long, collecting cans outran the label processing; the labels stayed on the cans, unsorted and uncounted. Butch began storing the dirty empty cans, with their labels still on, in trash bags stacked in the carport.

The neighbors began to notice.

Chapter 9. Church Life

Butch and his family had attended the big Presbyterian Church in Phoenix for years. Both he and Deena had participated in the youth programs and choir, and were known by nearly all the members. Although Jim didn't attend as regularly as the rest of the family, especially during horse racing season, he had also had held layman positions in the church over the years.

After Butch's accident, the church was a great comfort to the family as the long recovery project began. As Butch slowly progressed toward more normal functionality, his mental capacity was clearly not keeping up. As kids will do, some of the younger children would tease Butch, and make fun of him, but as Jessica said once, "Bless his heart, he doesn't even seem to notice. He just loves everyone." And everyone loved him.

After church, Butch delighted in meeting members, particularly the older ones. They also liked the way he treated them, helping them to their cars, or helping them carry things to the occasional potluck dinner.

Butch also had another activity after church. He kept an empty trash bag folded up in his pocket so that he could go back into the church kitchen to mine empty soup cans from the trash. Since everyone at church was rooting for Butch's recovery, his collecting activities didn't bother anyone, and several friends actually pitched in and helped.

So Elmer's trunk was nearly always full, even on weekends. And, of course, the driveway collection area continued to expand.

Chapter 10. Losing Elmer

Butch drove Elmer nearly every day, and nearly every day Elmer would come home with some dings and scratches. In the beginning, Jim would have them fixed, but they were all below the insurance deductible, and it began to be an annoying expense. It was also apparent to Jim that if the insurance company really knew how many minor accidents Butch had, the insurance would (and should) be much more expensive.

More worrisome, however, was that Jim and Jessica began to fear that Butch would have a more serious accident. Butch's driving skills didn't seem to be improving, and it might be only a matter of time before they were going to regret letting Butch have the car.

They discussed the problem with Butch's therapists and psychologists, to come up with a plan that would minimize Butch's distress at losing Elmer.

Unfortunately, in the meantime, Butch had a slightly more serious accident. Driving out of the church parking lot one Sunday, Butch was ogling a pretty girl when he ran smack into the side of Mr. Austin's brand new Cadillac.

Mr. Austin had known Butch all his life, and knew what the circumstances were. He wasn't mad at Butch, but clearly he should not be the one to pay for the damage to his own car. Now Jim and Jessica were faced with an insurance claim for someone else's vehicle, and one that was obviously not going to be the last.

So it had to be done.

After dinner that night, Jessica brought the subject up. "Butch, honey, you know we've got to get Mr. Austin's car fixed."

"Sure, Mom, I can take care of it. I'll sell some of my coins," Butch replied.

"No," Jim responded, "that won't do it. It will cost way more than that. We'll have to call the insurance company, and they will pay for it."

"Well, that's a lot better idea," said Butch.

"But that's not the only problem," Jessica added. "Honey, I just don't think you are going to be able to keep Elmer."

Butch's face went blank. What did she just say? It soaked in gradually.

"No, that's silly," Butch said. "I won't give up Elmer. If he goes, I'll go with him."

"No," Jim said, "That doesn't make any sense. Tell you what. We'll sell Elmer to someone who will take good care of him, and when you improve enough so you don't hurt him all the time, we'll get him back."

Butch thought about that for a minute.

"Will he be where I can visit him?" Butch asked.

"Oh, brother," Jim thought, "What next?"

"We don't know," Jessica ventured, "Maybe so, but probably not." Suddenly she thought of a way out.

"Don't you think it hurts Elmer every time you run into something?" she asked.

Now it was Butch's turn to think.

Jim got the message. "You know, it could be that Elmer would be better off somewhere else. I'm sure he would have fond memories of you. And you've got Little Elmer to remember him by."

Butch thought about the little yellow Mustang model on his bedroom shelf.

"How will I get around to my errands? How will I collect my soup cans?" Butch asked.

"Good sign," thought Jim, "Change the subject."

"How about a bike?" Jim asked.

"Red?" asked Butch.

"Of course," said Jessica, with some relief showing in her voice.

"When?" asked Butch.

"Tomorrow," replied Jim, "We'll go shopping tomorrow."

"And I'll find a nice home for Elmer," Jim added, wondering if this problem had gone away.

"Oh, no!" exclaimed Butch.

"Wait," Jessica said, "We have a deal. A red bike in return for Elmer. A new red bike. And Elmer's getting pretty beat up, you know. I think he needs to rest. And you can ride your bike all day, and even take the bus if you need to go farther."

"Well, that's right," thought Butch. He had memorized all the bus routes that went everywhere he wanted to go before he got Elmer, and he still remembered them.

"Well, OK," Butch replied, "Red and new."

It turned out that Butch couldn't master the bicycle, even after many tries. So they traded it in for a three-wheeler. Red. With baskets in front and back.

Chapter 11.   Losing Deena

Deena was living her dream life by now, having graduated from the University of Arizona and moved to Davis, California to get her veterinary degree from UC Davis. She was married now, and she and Mark were planning to start a family.

She kept in touch with her Phoenix family, particularly interested in Butch's progress. She had studied brain injuries, and knew the struggles he faced every day. It was clear to her that his progress had leveled off, leaving him about where he was before middle school, both intellectually and emotionally. It saddened her to think of the promise her little brother had that now was lost.

One night she and Mark were driving home from a friend's home after dinner. There was a severe rain storm arriving, and flash flood warnings were already being broadcast.

Both of them were sober, and Mark was not driving fast in the dark downpour. But when the car went through a dip in the country road, it hit some running water, hydroplaned, and slid sideways off the road.

The car hit a telephone pole that impacted right into the door on the passenger's side of the car. It crushed Deena's right thigh very badly. Most other injuries to the two of them were minor.

The surgeons did their best, but now, after many surgeries, Deena's right leg was shorter than the left, and she was facing the fact that her life was changed in many ways. She was athletic in addition to being intellectual, and cheerleading and dancing had been an important part of her life.

While mending in the hospital, she was surprised to find that she was newly pregnant. This was news that they welcomed, even though the family addition was going to happen a little sooner than they had planned. Deena could continue her studies as she began the rehab process, even though her pregnancy had begun.

However, she was very depressed about her leg, and visualized herself limping rather than dancing. The doctors prescribed an anti-depressant. Like Butch, these drugs helped Deena become more accepting of their life change.

In spite of the drugs, or, who knows, maybe because of them, Deena began to worry about her future health. She had read in medical journals about injuries like hers, and was concerned about the possibility of materials from the injury, bone crumbs, as she visualized it, entering her blood stream and travelling to her lungs or brain.

She became obsessed with this fear, to the point at which she decided that she needed to go home to Phoenix for a while to seek family comfort and help.

Now the family in Phoenix was whole again, with Butch living in his room and Deena back in her room. But the family was changed, as together they tried to cope with problems they had never expected to face. The exciting, bright hopes for the future they had before had been replaced with a somber, troubled effort at coping with their drastically-altered future.

As Butch continued his collecting of stuff, Deena sank lower and lower into a depressed state filled with worry and dread. Jessica and Jim tried their best to help.

"Mom," Deena said one evening before bed, "What if I'm disabled after my baby is born? What if my baby loses its mother?"

"Oh, honey," Jessica replied, "Don't worry about such things. You will be fine. I just know you will be a wonderful mommy, so let's just look forward to everything. You've got the best doctors. Just trust them."

Butch would often accompany Deena to one of the local college or public libraries where Deena would research her condition. Deena would pore over the medical journals, unwittingly convincing herself that she was facing disability or death from her leg injury. As her uncle Roger commented, "She is too smart for her own good in this case. She can't see that her worry and her research are confirming her fears."

One Saturday Uncle Joseph and Ann scheduled a family barbeque out at their big house on the edge of town, located on the edge of a date palm grove. It was a big Spanish hacienda, with several guest bedrooms upstairs. Joseph's home law office was downstairs, which he used in addition to the one that he and Roger shared downtown.

Like many lawyers, Joseph kept a revolver in his top right-hand desk drawer. Deena knew about the gun, but had no idea how to use it. She outwitted Joseph.

"Uncle Joseph," she said, "Mark and I are nervous living in the country like we do, and I'm alone a lot there. I was wondering if you could teach me how to use a weapon, so I can get one at home and know how to use it."

"Sure," Joseph replied, "It's easy. Let's go out back and have a lesson."

So they took the gun and some bullets out into the back yard, where Joseph taught Deena loading, unloading, checking, cleaning, basic safety, and, of course, shooting the gun. Joseph stuck pieces of paper onto the side of a big palm tree, and they used it as a target.

After the lesson, Deena helped clean the gun, re-load it, put the safety on, and replace it in the desk drawer.

Butch had gone fishing with a friend of his, in hopes of bringing back some fish to add to the barbeque. Joseph joined Roger and Jim talking man stuff while the ladies got side dishes prepared in the kitchen.

"Mom, I'm tired," Deena said. "I'm going to go upstairs for a nap. Is that OK?"

"Sure, honey," Jessica replied, "We'll wake you up when it's time to eat."

"I love you, Mom."

"I love you, too, honey"

On the way upstairs, Deena stopped by Joseph's dark office. Quietly, she opened the desk drawer and removed the loaded revolver. Tucking it under her arm, she limped up the stairs, lay down on the bed, covered her head with a pillow, and pulled the trigger.

BANG

Butch's face broke into a sheepish grin as he fumbled his end of the aluminum boat onto the concrete boat ramp.

"You're trying to kill the fish with a sonic boom?" laughed Ron.

"I'm sorry," Butch replied, "I hope it didn't hurt the boat."

"Naw, what's another dent or two in this old bucket? But at least we've got some fish today."

Butch carried the cooler with the fish into Joseph's kitchen, where Jessica and Ann were ready to start preparing them.

"Butch, honey," Jessica said, "We'll be eating in about half an hour. Would you mind going upstairs and waking up Deena? She's been napping for the last couple of hours."

Butch climbed the stairs, knocked lightly on the bedroom door, and didn't get a response. Gently, he opened the door, and saw Deena lying on the bed with the pillow over her head. Goofy way to sleep, he thought, and gently touched her shoulder. She didn't respond, so he lifted the pillow.

The shock and horror of what he saw was to stay with Butch for the rest of his life. Wordlessly, his eyes and mouth wide open, he staggered backwards until he backed into a dresser, knocking over the photos and startling himself with the racket.

Still speechless, he staggered out of the room to the top of the staircase, and yelled for help.

Butch was inconsolable. It was all a blur. A nightmare. The flashing red lights, the noise, the crying. The unanswerable question: Why?

It was up to Jessica to telephone Mark, who immediately came over to join the family in its sadness, confusion, and mourning. He had no more insight as to what had happened than any of them.

The psychiatrist on Butch's rehab team increased his medicine in an attempt to help him cope with the loss of Deena. Butch was haunted by the vision of what he had seen, and could not escape the horror and sadness that overwhelmed him.

To Butch, the funeral and burial seemed outside of his real world; as though he was a spectator to an event of which he was not a part. It was perhaps some sort of defense mechanism that enabled him to attend without dissolving into a sobbing blob.

But later, every night, he thought about Deena. And Amy, and Elmer. And he cried himself to sleep.

And the Mourning Dove sympathized with him, and sang him its mournful song: Coo-ah, coo, coo, coo. Coo-ah, coo, coo, coo.

Chapter 12.   The Briefcase

After a month or two, Jim and Jessica decided that
they needed to go on a short road trip with Butch to
try to get all of their minds off of what had
happened. Mark had returned to his and Deena's
home in California, where with the rest of his
family he tried to come to grips with the loss of
Deena.

Jessica suggested a trip to the Grand Canyon, one of
their favorite places. Butch agreed that it would be a
good trip, especially if they could go through Oak
Creek Canyon on the way. Oak Creek held many
happy memories for all of them there. Butch and
Deena would explore up and down the creek, its
clear cold water and lush vegetation a stark contrast
to the desert that surrounded their home.

Back then, Butch and Deena would go fishing in the
creek early in the morning, and come home with a
few trout for breakfast. Jim and Jessica would have
a warm fire started in the cabin's iron stove, and
coffee already brewing. Fresh pan-fried trout and
eggs. What a treat!

Today, as they drove north through Sedona, Butch
sat in the back seat holding his precious briefcase
on his lap. Except for his soup can expeditions, the
briefcase was his constant companion, usually
holding a supply of Arizona Highway magazines,

and maybe a Playboy, plus some coin collecting newsletters.

They passed through Sedona, and at the mouth of the canyon crossed Midgley Bridge. When they were little, Butch and Deena would erupt in laughter as they crossed "Midgley Bridgley" as they had named it. But today it nearly made Butch cry.

A few hours later they were at the Canyon, unloading their car into the cabin they had rented for the weekend. Butch carried his briefcase into the cabin also. It was unusually light, because he had carefully emptied it the night before they left home.

They had dinner in the big old rustic lodge near the South Rim of the Canyon. It was too dark to see anything in the canyon at this hour. (Another story that always broke the kids up in laughter was about the tourist who once asked if they lit the Canyon at night.) Trying to be as normal as they could, it was nonetheless very hard to carry on routine conversations while realizing that Deena was not with them.

Over the past month, all their friends and relatives had expressed their sorrow to them, and some, who would ask "Why would God let this happen?" and "We don't understand God's actions, but they must be accepted" puzzled Butch. He knew the answer. Why couldn't they?

44

He had figured it out when he was six. He had found a baby bird, naked and dying, lying on the back porch step. He had picked it up and brought it into the house crying. The bird had fallen out of a nest that had been under the eaves above the steps, and the ruined nest lay nearby.

Butch had told the story the next week in Sunday school, and his teacher, not wanting him to doubt God, explained to him that it could not be understood. God was good, and if the baby bird fell out of the nest and died there must be a reason. But Butch could not believe that the little bird had done anything wrong. He didn't deserve to die.

Butch struggled with this, and soon came up with his own theory. God created everything, including the baby bird, and loved everything as well. But God was too big and powerful to handle all the details. Creating everything and getting it all running was work at a very high level, Butch sensed, and even God could not save every little bird.

God saw the little bird and cried also, Butch believed. Of course God was sad. Just like we were. Now Butch felt better. Not only was he sad, God was, too.

At dinner that night at the Canyon, Butch decided that that also applied to Deena, and, by golly, even to his own plight. No blame, just sadness. He shared this view of things with his mother and dad that night, and after he was done they held hands and prayed. Glances between Jim and Jessica reflected their wonder and approval with Butch, because even *they* felt better believing that God cried for Deena.

After breakfast the next day, Butch left Jim and Jessica in the cabin working on a jigsaw puzzle to go for a walk. They did not notice that he had his briefcase with him.

He wasn't going to get better. Butch himself could see that. As optimistic as the therapists tried to be, Butch clearly was not going to ever live a normal life. He walked down the curving path toward the rim, idly kicking pinecones off the path as he walked. The sun hadn't been up long, but already the pine trees were warm enough to give off their pleasant smell.

Butch got to the rim just as the beams from the rising sun were beginning to illuminate the mesas and gorges below. The river, a mile below at the bottom of the canyon was still in darkness, but the opposite rim was resplendent in its shades of reds, browns, and whites.

He remembered simpler days. Sunrise at the Canyon. He remembered the whole family at home, getting up early on Easter morning, and tuning the radio to KTAR to listen to the sunrise service that would be broadcast from the South Rim of the Canyon. Howard Pyle, with his golden voice and genius for choosing words, would describe the scene as the sunlight crept over the east end of the Canyon and gradually begin to illuminate the chasm below. His words painted beautiful pictures in a thousand minds that were tuned in to the broadcast.

Then, after the sunrise service was over, the family would run outside for the Easter egg hunt before getting ready for church.

Where did it all go? Why was everyone so happy then and so sad now? He knew he was supposed to be a lawyer by now, working with his uncles downtown in the Luhrs Tower. It was clear now that that would never happen.

Butch stepped to the rail and looked over the edge at the dark, seemingly bottomless canyon below. Like the famous Greek statue of the discus thrower, he crouched, spun, and lofted the briefcase high in the air over the canyon. Now in sunlight, its shiny light brown leather glinted as it tumbled. Down and down it went, until it disappeared into the shadows below.

Butch sat down and began to cry.

Chapter 13.   The Harringtons

Recovery for everyone was slow, and for Butch it was months before he even got back to his collecting chores. And by then there was emerging another irritant. A thorn in Butch's side that would not go away: the Harringtons next door.

All of the neighbors loved Butch, and felt sorry for his plight. They, too, saw that his recovery was slowing, and resigned themselves that Butch would become a neighborhood character they would see coming and going on his red three-wheeled bike, with its baskets filled with junk.

But the neighbors right next door, the Harrington's, were the ones that faced the growing mess in Butch's driveway. And to make matters worse, the trash bags full of unwashed (and still labeled) soup cans began to smell, which was particularly noticeable when the wind came from the wrong direction.

Frank Harrington was away from the house most of the time at work, but Edith was at home nearly all the time, right next to Butch's collection of junk, as she called it. For months she had tried to get something done about it, but solutions always seemed to be temporary. Sure, a lot of it was moved to the back yard, but over time the now smaller collection in the driveway would grow again. And the back yard smelled, also.

Frank tried to keep Edith calm, but she became adamant as she recognized that things were not going to change next door for a long time. Several times she had asked Jessica to do something, often even in Butch's presence. Butch knew about the Harrington's displeasure, and took it personally. He didn't think his stuff was unsightly. He tried to keep the bags neatly stacked and the newspapers tied in bundles. To him it was his office, and his job was keeping it organized while it grew.

"If I wanted to live next door to the dump," Edith said one day, "I would move downtown."

Edith began legal proceedings to force the cleanup. Several times she tried, but Butch's uncles, combined with a sympathetic judge, kept thwarting her efforts.

Of course her efforts put an increasing strain on the relationship between the two families, and Butch was aware of that. Possibly he didn't fully understand his fault in the situation, because to him his stuff was his life, his career. The piles were not unattractive to him.

He didn't complain about them; why didn't they leave him alone?

Chapter 14.   Windstorm

One night, during the Monsoon season, a thunderstorm raged through their part of town. The whirling winds broke branches off of trees, and even took the roof off of the sheds next to the gas station over on the highway.

Butch's collection of newspapers had grown a great deal over the last couple of years, and he had them carefully stacked in the carport organized by date. Each stack of papers had a rock on top, but tonight's winds were too powerful.

When the top of one of the stacks blew off, the papers underneath began peeling off one after the other. And then more stacks began blowing, and pretty soon the carport was nearly empty of newspapers.

When neighbors arose the next morning, their entire neighborhood was covered with papers. Plastered around tree trunks, embedded in bushes, and scattered across lawns were dozens, maybe hundreds of papers and shreds of papers. Everyone knew immediately where the papers had come from.

A few of the neighbors simply got to work cleaning up the papers. Some even returned some papers to Butch, who was frantically trying to recover as many papers as he could, by himself. Some simply trashed the papers considering them a nuisance.

But the Harringtons did not take it well.

Jessica could hear Edith before she even got to the door.

"Edith," Jessica pleaded, "calm down. We'll clean it all up. Just give us a little time."

"My book club is coming over this morning, and they will think I live in a dump," Edith replied.

"We'll work as fast as we can," Jessica responded. "Jim and I are helping him. And we'll make sure this can't happen again."

And it didn't happen again. Jim brought home some concrete blocks for the papers that were left, and they never blew away again. But, of course, there was more to Butch's collection than just papers.

It was never clear whether the cat was a peace offering or a mean stunt. But it definitely did not work out the way Butch expected.

Chapter 15.   The Cat

One day Butch was pedaling his way back toward home, with his daily haul of soup cans and other treasures he had found. It had been a pretty good day, and both the front and rear baskets were nearly full. Plus, he had spotted something glittering in the sun, and he found an especially pretty piece of broken glass, purple when you looked through it, but kind of bluish in reflected light. He sat for a long time admiring it. He found a place for it in the rear basket and continued his trip home.

As he rounded a corner, he saw the cat lying in the road about a half a block away. As he got nearer, he noticed that the cat didn't run away. He stopped his bike and kneeled down beside the cat, and saw that the cat was dead; hit by a car probably.

He gently stroked its fur, soft and warm from the sunshine. It couldn't stay here, in the middle of the street. He made a nest for the cat in his front basket and curled it up there as though it was asleep.

When he got home, he parked his bike in its usual spot and began unloading the day's yield of treasure. Everything had a place; glass shards in one box, soup cans in the least-full bag, and the folded cardboard stuck in between a soup bag and the house wall. When all was done, he made an indentation in top of one of the trash bags, found an old towel for a lining, and laid the cat in the nest.

He wasn't sure what to do with the cat, but he couldn't have left it in the road, could he? And it was still soft and warm, as though it was just asleep.

Then he had a plan – a peace offering. He would give the cat to the Harringtons.

So that night he bundled the cat up in a soft towel, took it next door, and laid it on the doorstep.

The reaction was not what he had expected.

This incident resulted a few weeks later in a court order demanding that Butch stay off of the Harrington's property. Jessica did her best to explain to Butch about the rule, and he agreed that it was important to obey the law. He didn't like the Harringtons, especially after their reaction to the cat incident, but there was still enough memory of his lawyer ambitions to know that he had to do what he was told.

"Can I still walk on the sidewalk?" Butch asked.

"Yes, honey, but please stay off their lawn, or front walk or their driveway," Jessica replied.

Soon after, Butch walked down the sidewalk, paused in front of the Harrington's house, and after glancing around, stepped onto the lawn with his left foot. Then, with a grin on his face, he continued his walk down the sidewalk.

Other demands, having to do with the elimination of Butch's mess, were delayed for a long time. Jim, after all, had two brothers that were attorneys, and, making things even more difficult for the Harringtons, was that Judge McIntosh lived across the street. The judge had known Butch's family for more than 15 years, and was saddened by Butch's situation as much as anyone. So when the Harringtons pushed for action, the judge didn't go out of his way to work around the delaying actions of Roger and Joseph.

Of course, that couldn't last forever.

Chapter 16.   Losing Dad

One day Butch came home from his expeditions to find Jessica and Jim huddled together in the living room in a deep, quiet conversation. As Butch approached, they both looked up with fear and sadness in their eyes. Butch could tell something was wrong.

"Mom, Dad, are you OK?" Butch asked.

"Well, honey," Jessica replied, "Not really. Your dad is sick, and he got a bad report from the doctor today. But I'm sure he will be OK."

"Dad," Butch said, peering closely at Jim, "you look fine to me."

"Son, it doesn't show, at least not yet," Jim replied.

"When will you get well?" Butch asked.

"We don't know," replied Jessica, "Your dad has cancer, and the doctor says it is going to get bad fast. Of course the doctor might be wrong, so let's hope and pray for Dad to get well. But if he's right, we should know pretty soon."

But before long Jim was missing work, and, what was worse for Butch, one Friday Jim couldn't devote the day to Butch as he had for so long. Butch became very worried and depressed, and so Butch's medication had to be increased.

Butch now dreaded each day, and suffered through each night. Long ago, he had recovered Amy's picture from his wastebasket, and it now sat on one of his shelves beside his favorite photo of Deena. Beside Deena's photo was his little yellow Mustang model. All he had left was images. The girls and his car were gone. And now Dad might leave him?

He curled up on his bed and tried to think of other things.

And he listened as his Mourning Dove outside his window sang its sweet song.

Chapter 17.   The Dogs

There were five of them, and they stopped trotting a few houses away and sniffed the air. It was about three in the morning, and the full moon lighted the neighborhood with a soft eerie glow.

The dog's noses were their guides as they headed straight for Butch's driveway stash. The unwashed soup cans acted as bait for the dogs, and they sniffed about until they identified the black plastic trash bags as the source of the scent.

One dog attempted to take off with a bag, but it ripped as he ran, leaving a trail of soup cans behind him. Two other dogs started a fight over another bag, tearing it into shreds. The plastic shreds caught the breeze and sailed silently into the night, where they wrapped themselves around the Harrington's trees and shrubs.

Another dog ran gleefully down the street, leaving behind empty soup cans clattering down the pavement.

The racket woke up the neighborhood, and one at a time porchlights went on. One of the neighbors started yelling at the dogs, which woke up anyone not already awake.

Butch woke up, rubbed his eyes, and listened, trying to figure out what was going on. He got out of bed, and looked out the window. What he saw, the dogs ripping up and scattering his soup can collection, enraged him.

Wearing only his pajama bottoms, he raced out of the house, passing Jessica who was headed to the front window to see what was going on. Jim heard the racket, but couldn't get out of bed, so he listened intently trying to figure out what was going on.

Butch joined the fray outside, trying to take what was left of a bag out of the nearest dog's mouth. Of course the dog thought they were playing, and started a tug of war that resulted in more tears in the bag and more cans scattered over the yard.

Meanwhile a few other neighborhood dogs joined in with the strays, having the time of their lives. Even those who couldn't get out of their yards joined in, by barking along with the others.

Butch was yelling at the dogs through his tears, trying to get them to go away, and at the same time trying to pick up some loose cans into a bag that was already too torn up to hold them. It was a hopeless, frantic scene, and one that was not amusing to anyone.

"This," thought Edith Harrington, "is the last straw."

And as Judge McIntosh witnessed the whole scene through his front window, sighed and shook his head. "Yes," he thought, "the time has come to end this. Perhaps I can help prepare Butch. And I wonder how Jessica can cope, with Jim in such bad shape."

Chapter 18.   Losing Stuff

Neighbors were helping to clean up the mess, but Edith was already in the living room facing Jessica, demanding that this must be over. Fortunately, Judge McIntosh joined them, whose presence brought some semblance of calm and order.

Butch was outside gathering cans and plastic scraps, so the three of them could express themselves freely. The judge explained what all of them knew; they all loved Butch, and were sorry for his condition. But Jessica, perhaps with the help of the rehab staff, must change Butch's objectives. He had to stop collecting junk.

Jessica faced that order with fear knotting her stomach. She knew Butch better than anybody. He wasn't going to stop wanting to collect things. That had been planted in his brain since it had started healing. It was part of him. Like his arms and legs, it was now an integral part of his very being.

Jessica needed help, so later in the day she called the clinic. One doctor she talked to didn't seem to grasp the situation. "Just call a junk dealer" was all he had to say. Finally, working her way through the psychiatric department, she found a senior nurse who had known Butch for years. She knew this was not going to be easy.

For the next several days, they gradually increased Butch's medication. His reaction to losing his stuff couldn't be predicted by anyone, even Jessica. But he was tall and strong, and she knew he could hurt her even though it might be by accident. She had witnessed his disappointments over the years, and had seen him in a sudden rage before lapsing into sadness and quiet depression.

Jessica and the staff worked out a plan. The truck would come while Butch was going through the trash at the old folks' home so that he wouldn't be able to confront the workers as they loaded the truck. They also managed to have two husky orderlies on hand in the house in case Butch got violent. They would also be equipped with tranquilizing needles to use if necessary.

The day came, and Butch left according to his usual schedule. He normally would not return for two hours, which left plenty of time for the truck to arrive and get loaded. However, when Butch arrived at his third stop, workmen were resurfacing the roadway, and he couldn't get to the last set of dumpsters.

Butch, with his tricycle only half full today, headed home an hour earlier than usual.

The truck had arrived on time, and the workers lost no time in getting the truck loaded. After loading the truck, they swept the driveway, got in the truck, and started the engine. Butch rounded the corner in time to see the truck pulling out of the driveway, and, glancing at the now clean pavement in the carport, suddenly realized what had happened.

As the truck pulled away, Butch started after it, pedaling as hard as he could. The workmen saw Butch in the rear view mirror, and having been told of the situation, realized that this was not according to plan. They accelerated the truck, realizing that no good could come of confronting Butch.

Butch cried and yelled, but the truck outran him, and he had to give up the pursuit, exhausted and broken. He saw a few glass shards that had fallen off the truck, and he stopped to pick them up.

Jessica, who had seen the truck leave, was shocked to see Butch appear out of nowhere and begin chasing the truck. Watching through the kitchen window, with the orderlies watching over her shoulder, she saw Butch slowly making his way back toward the house, stopping now and then to recover some remains of his collection.

By the time he parked his bike in the newly clean carport, he was a mess. He was both enraged and saddened. Both emotions were boiling over. He had nothing left.

He burst into the kitchen, and ignoring the orderlies and Jessica pulled open the knife drawer and tried to pick up a butcher knife. The orderlies pounced, to stop him. The struggle intensified as Butch, already strong, seemed to have energy and strength beyond normal. Butch cut himself groping in the drawer, and within seconds had bloodied himself and the orderlies. One of the orderlies finally managed to stab Butch in the thigh with the needle, and the two of them finally got Butch to the kitchen floor where they held him until the tranquilizer took effect.

Jessica watched all this in horror. How could it have come to this? How could their perfect lives have been transformed into the nightmare it has become? And now comes Jim, stumbling out of the bedroom, heavy with drugs, trying to comprehend the terrible scene before him.

They finally got Butch into his bed, cleaned him up, and the orderlies left. They promised to remain on call in case they were needed. They placed two plastic hospital bracelets on his wrist, so that whoever might come to help would know the recent medical history.

Butch didn't wake up until the next morning, when the Mourning Dove tried to console him with her soft, cooing, sad song.

Chapter 19.   Losing Butch

Butch woke up in a fog. What had happened? Why did he hurt? His head was pounding as he arose and headed for the bathroom. Splashing cold water on his face began to revive him, and he went back to his bedroom, dressed, and went out into the house.

He walked into the kitchen, and looked out the window at the clean driveway. He walked to the kitchen door, and looked out the window at the place where his stuff had been. He felt numb, as though he was living a nightmare and couldn't wake up.

He had nothing left, he thought. Even his dad was going to leave soon, getting sicker by the day. He heard a rustle behind him, and turned to see Jessica, still in her nightgown and bathrobe, walking toward him with tears in her eyes.

"Mom," Butch said, "why did you do this to me?"

"Honey," she replied, "we didn't want to. We had to. If we didn't, the sheriff would. The neighbors couldn't stand it anymore."

"Who cares about them," he said, "they all hate me."

"No, they don't hate you. It may seem that way, but they love you. They love you, but they can't stand your stuff in the driveway."

"We need to get my stuff back."

"Honey, it's not coming back."

"Ever?"

"No, not ever. I'm sorry, but that's the way it has to be."

A change seemed to come over Butch. Some kind of calm resignation fell on him like a soft blanket. He had a far-away look in his eyes as though he had made a decision, and was at peace with it.

Later in the day, while Jessica was at the market, Butch went into his parent's bedroom, where Jim lay sleeping. Butch put his hand on his father's shoulder for a moment, turned around, and picked up Jim's wallet that was lying on the dresser.

Butch opened the wallet, and fished out one of his dad's credit cards. Pocketing the credit card, he went into his room, and, sitting on his bed, went through his collection of Arizona Highway magazines to find his favorite issue. December. With the centerfold of the Grand Canyon dusted with a recent snowfall.

Butch checked his pocket money, rolled up the magazine, and left the house. He walked past his red tricycle, looked forlornly at the empty driveway, and walked three blocks to the corner bus stop.

The bus arrived that had the right route number, and he boarded the bus. The sign in the destination window of the bus said "Downtown."

As the bus made its way on its route, Butch looked at the photos in the magazine. Besides his favorite of the Canyon, he also loved the sunsets. The colors, especially if the picture included a silhouette of a cactus, were fascinating. The cactus needles catching the sunlight around the black silhouette made a golden glow, like a rim of fire. A cactus with a halo.

The bus was nearing downtown now, and Butch turned his attention to the street scene. He watched as the Luhrs Tower came into view, and spotted a young attorney walking down the street carrying a briefcase. He even had an attractive assistant walking with him. He watched them until they rounded the corner.

The bus stopped at the downtown station. Nearby were the typical places; a jail bond office, a pawn shop, and a gun store.

Butch walked into the gun store, and looked over the selection in the case. He saw one that looked like Uncle Joseph's, and decided that it would be a good choice.

"How much is that gun," he asked the young attendant.

"$250"

"OK, I'll take it. But I need some bullets," Butch said.

The attendant eyed Butch's hospital bracelets, and couldn't help noticing the one that said "Psychiatric Hospital" along with the hospital's name. Two plastic bracelets, one white and one red.

The attendant hesitated. It wasn't his shop, and he didn't make much money working there. His share of the sale would be nearly $50, and he could make a few more bucks on the ammunition. He had bills to pay, and the first of the month was not far away.

"How much ammo do you need?" asked the attendant.

"Just load it for me," said Butch. "I don't need a box."

"OK, I'll get it ready for you."

The attendant loaded the weapon, put it in a paper bag, and handed it to Butch. Butch pulled out his father's credit card and handed it to the attendant.

"I'll need to see some ID," the salesman asked.

Butch pulled out his driver's license, and hoped the attendant would not notice that he was "James, Jr." on the license and "James" on the credit card.

Maybe the attendant noticed, and maybe he didn't. In any case, he ran the card, returned it to Butch, and closed the register.

Butch walked back to the bus station, and while waiting for a bus home, folded the gun into the magazine and threw away the bag and receipt.

On the bus ride home, Butch sat and stared out the window, eyes open but not seeing. He was in a dream of some kind.

Jessica finished the dishes, wiped her hands on a towel, and turned away from the kitchen window. She headed for the bedroom to check on Jim, and just missed seeing Butch coming down the sidewalk. He stopped in front of his house, looking briefly at the empty carport before continuing on to the house next door.

Edith's kitchen was at the back of the house, with a view of the back yard instead of the front of the house. Fred was in the front of the house, in the living room reading the paper, when he noticed Butch coming down the sidewalk.

"Edith, Butch is coming over," he called out.

"Well, see what he wants," Edith replied. "Let me know if you need anything. I'll be out in a minute."

Edith heard the front screen door open.

And then she heard the shot.

71

She had grown up on a ranch, and she knew a gunshot when she heard it.

She held the dishtowel to her mouth, and wide-eyed looked to the doorway into the dining room. She couldn't see into the living room, but the light from the front window showed the shadow of a man coming toward the dining room.

She was paralyzed with fear. Had Butch shot Fred? Was she next? How could this happen?

Around the doorway appeared Fred, in shock, and unable to speak. Then he found the words.

"Butch shot himself on our front porch," he said, his voice trembling.

"Oh, God, no. No. No, please. Please no," was all she could say.

"Let's just stay here in the kitchen and I'll call Jessica," Fred said. "And I'll call the police, too."

"No," Edith replied, "it would be better if you let the police go to Jessica's after they get here."

And so, after all Butch had lost, we finally lost him.

Before the sirens started, the Mourning Dove, looking down at the sad scene, sang its last song to Butch: Coo-ah, coo, coo, coo. Coo-ah, coo, coo, coo.

Chapter 20.   Epilogue

Well, that's the story. As Jessica had wished, we hope that this story will save lives.

It's not as easy as it used to be to purchase hand guns, but the frequency of prescribed anti-depressants has increased over the years.

This story illustrates the dangers inherent in anti-depressants, and how they may be the catalyst for self-destructive behavior. People who are taking or who knows someone who is taking these drugs must be alert for any of the danger signs.

Jessica forever regretted not taking more seriously Deena's sadness, depression, and statements, and, of course, Butch's overwhelming sense of loss. Looking back, there are always clues, but it is easy to misinterpret them. The lesson is that those on anti-depressants must be monitored very closely.

If you or someone you know needs help, please call somebody. We list a few resources here, but don't overlook friends, church members, clergy, or people you know in the medical profession.

Local Emergency Services 911

National Suicide Prevention Hotline 1-800-273-8255

Veterans Crisis Hotline 1-800-273-8255

Treatment Advocacy Center 1-800-784-2433

You can also Google the phrase "suicide prevention" to get local numbers for your area.

To hear the song of the Mourning Dove, go to https://www.allaboutbirds.org/guide/Mourning_Dove/sounds.

Jim only lived a few months after Butch died, but Jessica lived 15 more years. Jim had been a good provider, and a good manager of the funds the family received on behalf of Butch, so at least she didn't have financial stress on top of the rest. Jessica lived alone in the house for several years, and then moved to a retirement home where we visited her now and then.

Jessica had a strong character, and must have had a tough time fighting off her own sadness. How her life and that of those she loved changed so drastically and so quickly – suddenly there would be no grandchildren around the Christmas tree, no birthday celebrations, and no expectation of great-grandchildren.

And then, one night she went to sleep and didn't wake up. And the last leaf on her branch of the family tree fluttered to the ground.

I'm sure she went to sleep to the soft, soothing sounds of the Mourning Dove.

www.ingramcontent.com/pod-product-compliance
Lightning Source LLC
Chambersburg PA
CBHW062016280526
45787CB00005B/2129